VANCOUVER
THE STORY AND THE SIGHTS

by

Barry Bondar

Whitecap Books
NORTH VANCOUVER, B.C., CANADA

BORN OF THE FOREST

FEW FORESTS IN the world could challenge these stands of Douglas-fir. Fed by Pacific rains, cradled by a moderate climate, and left unharvested for centuries, these ancient spires towered one hundred metres above the cool and damp of the forest floor. In a time of wooden ships, timber of this quality and size was valued worldwide.

It was on the strength of this timber that several small communities sprang up along the Burrard Inlet in the late 1860s. Each had its own unique character. Moodyville, the village across the water, was the quietest and most reserved of the towns. It could be described as the quintessential "company town," led by the strict dictates of the mill owner and his wife. Like Moodyville, the community of Hastings Mill was also centred around its lumber facilities. The residents, however, suffered fewer edicts from the owner. As a result, life was a little less reserved. Finally, there was Granville. It was a rowdy, boisterous, extroverted town quite happily remaining at the other end of the spectrum.

Granville had a saloon. So important was this institution that the street numbering system of the old town actually flowed from this centre of the community. Granville was unofficially known as "Gastown," after its best-known citizen, "Gassy"

The Burrard Inlet timber was known worldwide for its quality and great size.

Lumbering, 1896. Horses were used to haul logs along trails known as "skid roads."

Jack Deighton. Deighton's status, it is suspected, was highly influenced by the fact that he owned the local watering hole.

Despite the inherent differences in the character of each community, all were united in their distaste for the snooty, highbrow neighbor across the water—Victoria.

As Britain's first colony in the west, Vancouver Island had managed to consolidate its position as the economic and political powerhouse of the region. Unwilling to relinquish any of its authority, the island was less than supportive of the dreams of growth and development of the Burrard Inlet communities.

Particularly infuriating to the mainlanders was the fact that everything seemed to fall in Victoria's favour. When Britain amalgamated its Vancouver Island and mainland colonies into the united colony of British Columbia, for example, Victoria won the right to call itself the capital city, despite the fact that a mainland community had already held that honour for a year.

Understandably, frustrations of this sort established a rivalry between the mainland and Vancouver Island which was to last for decades. Victoria's gains also perpetuated an early attitude that Vancouver Island was destined for greatness, while the mainland communities would play only a secondary role in coastal events.

THE BATTLE FOR THE RAILWAY

TIMES WERE CHANGING. The British Empire no longer wished to support all of its colonies and in 1870, Britain released British Columbia with the suggestion that it join the Confederation of Canada. Many Vancouver Islanders loyal to Britain felt betrayed by the action, and seriously argued that B.C. join the United States. So vociferous were they that Canada agreed to build a transcontinental railway to link the west coast with the rest of the country. Buckling to intense lobbying by Victoria, Canada also agreed to bypass the Burrard Inlet communities, swing the railway north and construct a series of bridges to Vancouver Island so that the railway's western terminus would end in Victoria.

The mainland, long a supporter of Confederation, saw this decision as yet another example of Victoria's good fortune.

But as the railway neared completion, Canada found itself mired in an economic recession. The fragile country could not afford to extend the railway beyond the strait. It would have to end at Burrard Inlet. The news was to hit Victoria like a thunderbolt; the island residents were horrified. The mainlanders were jubilant—and with good reason: this single event, more than any other, marked a turning point in the fortunes of the rival communities and helped establish the character of each.

Drawing of "Gassy" Jack Deighton welcoming his patrons to the Globe Saloon.

4

Granville — June, 1885.

When word of this dramatic change in plans reached the Burrard Inlet, the entire region reacted with unrestrained enthusiasm. Port Moody, at the head of the inlet, was officially designated as the location for the terminus, but the other communities did not automatically accept this latest "official" declaration. Land speculation was rife and dozens of real estate offices sprang up overnight to deal with the burgeoning demand for any piece of property which might carry with it the prospect of prosperity. Railway executives watched the situation carefully and approached each community with the goal of achieving the best possible settlement. Negotiations were hard and land concessions were

great. Finally, in 1884, William Van Horne, vice-president of the C.P.R., made the long awaited and critical announcement.

Granville would greet the first locomotive from the east. It was an extraordinary coup for a town that had previously depended upon its saloon for prestige.

Granville eagerly grabbed at the dreams of growth and industrialization. The town grew at a furious pace and, in celebration of the bright and dynamic future offered by the railway, was officially renamed Vancouver in 1886 after the British captain who first charted the area in 1762.

DISASTER

VANCOUVER'S BIRTH WAS marred by tragedy. A mere two months after incorporation, the entire community was engulfed by clearing fires which had leapt out of control. One witness described the conflagration, saying, "Vancouver did not burn, it exploded."

So intense were the flames that, in a matter of only a few minutes, virtually no building remained

Vancouver after the fire of June 13, 1886. The Regina Hotel in the distance was one of the few buildings to escape destruction.

Vancouver. after. fire
Copyright applied for

intact. Yet even a disaster of this proportion could not dampen the promise of greatness. A tent city sprang into being and a spirit of renewal pervaded the ashen remains. The old, somewhat shabby, and disorganized town was lost forever. Residents looked forward to a new beginning for a new community.

On the very next day, Vancouver began to rise from the ashes.

Immediately after the fire, a "tent town" sprang up to house those people who were left homeless.

Real estate office, now the site of the Hudson's Bay store on Granville Street.

Arrival of the first transcontinental passenger train at the foot of Howe Street, May 23, 1887.

GROWING PAINS

LIFE WAS NOT ALL that easy in the new town. First, Victoria was still zealously protecting its economic interests, even refusing to purchase mainland products. Despite this ongoing irritation, Vancouver gradually lured an increasing number of industries. Yet even as the city accomplished its goal of increasing growth, the rapid rate of settlement mired the city in a number of problems. The "Pacific jewel" was very much a jewel in the rough.

As in all west coast communities, men far outnumbered women. Prostitution was common. Drinking was excessive. Everyone suffered the antics of the ubiquitous drunks and gamblers. Violence was an expected if unenviable fact of life. Corpses turned up regularly, some as a result of the dreaded typhus caused by unsanitary conditions, others from the bitter rivalries between various groups engaged in the lucrative opium trade that flourished in the early city.

The corner of Carrall and Powell streets, 1886.

Water Street looking east from Cordova, about nine months after the great fire of June 13, 1886.

Town planning was haphazard and the community struggled to maintain even the most basic of facilities. The sewage system was not initiated until 1888. As a result, water supplies were often tainted. Roads were usually simple trails which tended to turn into swamps when the rains came. There was little street lighting until the 1890s.

As was common during the Victorian era, distinctions between class and wealth led to distinct residential areas. Although the early residents who had made their fortunes in "Old Granville" tended to remain in the central hub of Vancouver, many of the newly arriving professionals and railway officials moved to exclusive residential areas along English Bay, nearer the ocean views and cleansing Pacific winds. Prior to Vancouver's boom, the wealthier citizens thus had a forest buffer zone—now the core of the city—between their homes and the commercial centre of Vancouver. It would not take long, however, before all of the forest of the peninsula would fall.

11

There was one factor which united all Vancouver residents no matter what their station in life. There was a mutual agreement to ignore the hardships of the young city as the unavoidable consequences of rapid growth. Pride in the community and faith in the future prevailed. Time would cure the ills. For the moment, all that mattered was that Vancouver should grow and expand its economic base. Better to think about polishing the "jewel of the Pacific" only when all its facets had been fully revealed.

Fortunately for Vancouver, the citizens had a symbol for the future: the spectacular beauty of 405-hectare Stanley Park, established in 1888. There was a general belief that someday the city would be a fitting setting for the natural wonder of this paradise.

(Opposite) The "Hollow Tree" was long a major attraction for those visiting Stanley Park.

Vancouver, 1887. Water Street looking west.

THE BOOM YEARS

VANCOUVER FOUND ITS most frantic pace around the turn of the century. In the span of a single decade, Vancouver had grown to completely dominate the fishing and lumber industries. An incredible three-quarters of the total provincial output now flowed from the young city. It was an extraordinary accomplishment considering that just a few short decades earlier Vancouver was looked upon as an unlikely successor to Victoria's crown.

Spurred by the Klondike gold rush of 1898—1903, Vancouver's boundaries expanded dramatically as thousands of people poured into the city on their way to the northern gold fields. There were so many new arrivals from Europe, eastern Canada, the United States and the Orient that not a single hotel or boardinghouse room remained vacant. Indeed, it was this influx of people from around the world which set the stage for Vancouver's distinctive cosmopolitan flair.

(Facing page) Burrard Inlet offered safe moorage for the great sailing vessels of the late 1800s. At the time of the lower photograph, ca. 1915, steamships were rapidly replacing the old masted vessels.

Hastings Street, ca. 1910—1915.

It was during this boom period that the C.P.R., using the vast tracts of land conceded to it during the negotiations of the 1880s, sought to create a new commercial district to the west of the "old Granville" district. Using the opulent Hotel Vancouver as bait, the C.P.R. succeeded in attracting new businesses and in luring established companies from the old commercial district. The rise of this new city core spelled disaster for the Granville district. The east end began a gradual decline which was not halted until the 1960s.

As immigration accelerated, the cocoon of Vancouver's peninsula grew too small to hold the burgeoning population. The boundaries of the city swept outward. New suburban communities proliferated and an intricate network of streetcar lines linked the new centres with the city core. The west end, once the exclusive centre for the more affluent, became a higher-density mix of people from all stations in life. Estates gradually gave way to apartment buildings. In turn, the C.P.R., ever responsive to demand, established a new exclusive district called Shaughnessy Heights.

As in any new city spurred by rapid growth, there were tensions. Housing and jobs were at a premium and minority groups tended to bear the brunt of market uncertainty. The ethnic diversity which is an important part of the sophisticated Vancouver of today was then considered a threat. The community had neither the social nor the emotional maturity to accept such diversity. This would come only later.

(Facing page) The C.P.R. depot and the C.P.R. Hotel Vancouver were used to lure businesses from the old city centre to C.P.R. lands. Both buildings have been subsequently replaced with newer structures.

The C.P.R. development of Shaughnessy Heights in 1912 was designed specifically for key personnel of the railway and for others of wealth and influence.

C.P.R. Hotel Vancouver,
Vancouver, B.C.

Just as the boundaries of the city expanded outward, the buildings began to stretch upward. A three-story limit was increased to an unprecedented ten floors. Even these limits were ignored. When completed in 1910, the thirteen-story Dominion Trust building was the tallest building in the British Empire. Promoted as "an object of pride" which represented "the most prosperous go-ahead commercial city on the continent," the new structure accurately reflected the bright future that all envisioned for Vancouver. As a result, it came as no surprise when only two years later, the seventeen-story Sun Tower stole the title of tallest building. What did cause some consternation was Toronto's arrogance in building a larger structure in 1914. Little did Vancouver realize that this loss was to presage a disastrous decline.

(Facing page) The Dominion Trust Building was once the tallest building in the British Empire and the highest steel structure on the west coast.

Banks and other leading business and commercial companies used massive pillars and columns to lend a sense of strength and permanence to their structures. The "iron-wedge" design of the Hotel Europe (above) was the distinguishing characteristic of one of the most opulent hotels in the city. It was one of the few early buildings to use fireproofing and was advertised as the "only absolutely fireproof hotel in the Dominion."

A NEW VISION

FOR ALL OF VANCOUVER'S apparent promise, a series of world events was about to shake a helpless city to its core. For the next three decades Vancouver would suffer economic depressions and recessions, labour strife, and the devastating effects of two world wars. Industries that had only begun to gain a foothold in what seemed a city of limitless opportunities were forced to retreat to more certain environments in the east. The torrent of commercial activity dwindled to a mere trickle.

Occasionally there were brief periods of growth to rekindle the dreams. The 1920s, for example, saw a major expansion of the port facilities to handle the increasing volumes of prairie grains. Public work projects, such as the construction of the City Hall and the Burrard Street bridge, helped add bold and dynamic structures to the city's skyline. Despite these additions, it was impossible to hide the general deterioration of the city. The people were hurting, and the extraordinary confidence and faith in the concept of growth that had once fired the city into life was now slipping through the cracks of decay and economic stagnation.

The 1930s found Vancouver at a crossroads in its evolution. In a subtle way, the magnificent Marine Building at 355 Burrard Street signalled this change. Designed in 1929, the building was described as "some great crag rising from the sea, clinging with flora and fauna, tinted in sea-green, touched with gold." It was as if the architects were capturing the early history of the city. Vancouver had indeed grown from an isolated lumber town to a magnificent city like some "great crag rising from the sea." And for the early residents, Vancouver's promise of growth and prosperity must have made it seem as though the city was truly touched with gold.

Vancouver skyline, 1936.

Looking down Hastings Street toward the Marine Building.

But dreams die hard. The builders who trusted in the continuation of growth were shattered by the depression of the thirties. People began to look beyond industrialization and commercialism. Cultural facilities such as the University of British Columbia, the Vancouver Symphony Orchestra, and the Vancouver Art Gallery jostled uneasily with Vancouver's characteristic bawdy pattern of life. Residents began to truly notice the spectacular physical beauty of the environment and demand that the city complement the physical beauty. The quality of life assumed a new importance.

Thus, when prosperity finally returned to Vancouver after the Second World War, the city did not respond with a drive for progress at any cost. Growth was clearly welcome, but it was no longer the soul of the city.

Vancouver had grown from the gangly, awkward stage of adolescence, with its need to prove itself. The problems associated with its youthful, unstructured growth and its disappointments with dreams turned sour had forged a new maturity. Rather than fear differences, the city began to nurture them, and the influx of postwar immigrants easily found a niche in the city. Their influence is seen in the distinctive European style of shops along Robson Street.

With the prosperous decades after the war came a new period of growth for Vancouver. The Vancouver skyline changed dramatically as towering new skyscrapers began to dominate the downtown core. In a few short years of building frenzy, many of the older buildings in the downtown and west end were obliterated. But soon residents of the city realized that unregulated building could destroy the character of the city, and a concerted effort was made to preserve the historic areas. Chinatown, Gastown and buildings in the downtown and west end areas were the subject of preservation and restoration programs, with the result that today Vancouver is an exciting mixture of old and new.

Vancouver, with its unparalleled natural setting, a remarkable balance of history and new development, and an attention to cultivation of distinctive communities, compares favorably with beautiful cities around the world. Instead of trying to create a homogeneous city, Vancouver encourages and celebrates its differences.

Celebration.....perhaps no other word captures the underlying nature of Vancouver so well.

English Bay beach area and the West End prior to the explosive growth of highrise apartments, ca. 1920—25.

GASTOWN

THE DAY WAS OVERCAST and drizzly, but this did not dampen the spirit of Mr. Jack Deighton. In September of 1867 he stepped ashore with a product that he knew would be looked upon as a salvation by tired, bored lumbermen—alcohol. Within a small grove of maples, the famous Globe Saloon was opened for business. It was an immediate success.

Dispensing both whisky and rather lengthy monologues, "Gassy" Jack set the tone for his drinking establishment. It was loud, boisterous and rowdy. So, too, was the town that grew up around the saloon. Granville, more affectionately known as "Gassy's town," readily adopted the characteristics of the Globe.

This unique character of the town not only permitted it to survive the devastating fire of 1886, but it also prepared it for the explosive growth that was to arrive with the railway. Like the saloon, the town spawned drive, ambition, and dreams.

The arrival of the railway marked a turning point for the town. As the first locomotive crawled to a halt, steam and cinders shrouded the engine. Noise from the crowd and the music of the local band fused into a cacophony of sound. Dignitaries paced as they waited their opportunity to deliver well-rehearsed speeches. The air buzzed with excitement and anticipation. It was a new beginning.

Vancouver exploded into activity. Warehouses seemed to appear overnight in an effort to support shipping and transportation. Forests to the east and west fell rapidly to make room for a population that would triple to 15,000 in only five years. Rooming houses and hotels could not be constructed fast enough to support the ever increasing transient population. The town frantically tried to keep pace with demands for water, sewage lines, street lamps and electric streetcars.

With the exception of a brief recession in the 1890s the town grew at an extraordinary pace, boosted by the Klondike gold rush at the turn of the century. Buildings grew larger and higher; hotels became more opulent. The old Gastown became the commercial hub of the new metropolis, a natural evolution.

But the situation changed almost overnight. The C.P.R. wished to develop its own vast holdings of land conceded to it during railway negotiations.

Statue of Jack Deighton located in Gastown.

Gastown holds some of the oldest structures of the city. This building was constructed in 1898 and originally served as a ship chandlery and hardware business.

Using several beautiful new buildings as lures, the railway attempted to create a new, bolder alternative to the Gastown commercial centre; the gamble was successful. New businesses chose to settle in the west, and Gastown began a slow decline. As the economic depression following the First World War settled upon the entire city, Gastown plunged into oblivion.

During the following difficult three decades of depression, Gastown became home for less fortunate citizens. Though shabby and run-down, the area seemed frozen in time, retaining a turn of the century flavour.

When prosperity returned, Gastown was recognized as a prime target for urban renewal. Today, we can enjoy the benefits of this enlightened approach which combines faithful rehabilitation of heritage buildings with the most up-to-date shops, art galleries, and restaurants. It is an intriguing area, where past and present meet.

THE DOWNTOWN CORE

WILLIAM VAN HORNE was troubled. Preliminary surveys for the western terminus had recommended that the community of Port Moody be the site for the railway terminus. When Van Horne surveyed the area for himself in August of 1884, he realized that the town's location was simply not adequate. There was an insufficient amount of land to build a metropolis, and the costs for reclaiming the tidal marshes for the railway would be millions of dollars. His eyes were set upon the lands around the town of Granville.

Knowing that the government would be more than willing to agree to the relocation and the funding of the railway extension in order to spur the sale of public lands, Van Horne took a hard line in negotiations. After all, he had the Port Moody location safely tucked away in his back pocket.

In his discussions with the provincial premier, he demanded one half of the entire peninsula upon which Vancouver now sits. He settled for an outright grant of 2,428 hectares along with the land concessions from the communities of Granville and Hastings Mill. It was upon these lands that most of the important downtown development occurred.

As you travel through the downtown core, look for the clues which reveal several distinct development phases. Phase one began soon after the great fire of 1886, when most businesses rebuilt in old Granville. Only a few of the relatively squat, small buildings of the period are found outside Gastown—most are located along the 400- and 500-block of West Hastings Street.

(Facing page) The Canada Pavilion is one of the newest additions to the waterfront. The teflon sails and unique "ship" design provide a striking addition to the city's skyline.

Both the sails of Canada Pavilion, to the right, and the dome of the stadium, to the left, are captured in this aerial of downtown Vancouver.

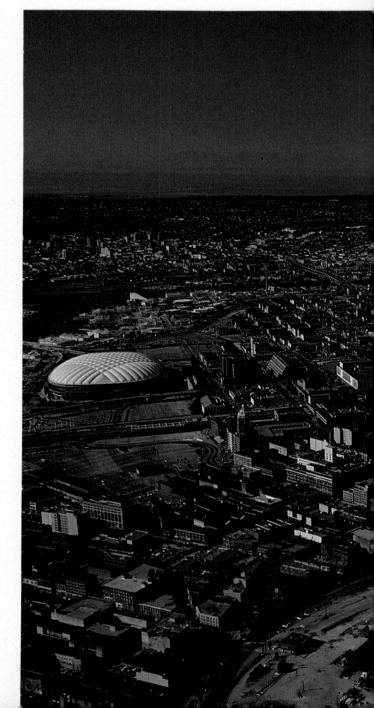

The Marine Building reflected in the modern glass and steel towers offers a beautiful contrast in archictectural styles.

Vancouver's old courthouse was refurbished and redesigned to house the Vancouver Art Gallery.

The law court buildings, created by Arthur Erikson, are designed to promote greater openness and accessibility of the legal system to the general public.

Phase two—the explosive development during the boom years at the turn of the century—is readily apparent. There are many buildings of the period in the eastern part of the downtown core. Constructed of sandstone and granite, they often have huge exterior columns which lend an air of permanence and strength. Marble was used liberally in interiors and open, expansive rotundas and foyers were often used to greet clients upon entering the building.

After the financial crash of the 1920s, construction in the city core slowed to a crawl. Those few buildings of this third phase tend towards massive brick behemoths which tower over the surrounding older granite and sandstone neighbors. As was fashionable during this period, the brick buildings were draped in swaths of coloured terra cotta decorations. The Marine Building is an example.

Vancouver's most recent expansionist phase began after the Second World War. Fortunately for the city, the modern steel and glass skyscrapers which have filled the skyline have not been designed solely upon the traditional box shape. Corporations, land developers, city planners, and the public have worked diligently to ensure that the city skyline matches the beauty and diversity of the surrounding landscape. As a result, the downtown area contains a fascinating array of innovative, modern architecture.

Vancouver is fortunate in that many examples of heritage buildings remain in use and this diversity of architecture from all stages of the city's evolution creates a distinctive and dynamic city core.

CHINATOWN

THOSE FORTUNATE enough to experience the Chinese New Year celebrations will have a memorable introduction to the second largest Chinese and Asian community in North America. From the swirl of the yellow and scarlet robes and banners, and the winding, snaking dance of the dragon, to the delicacies served in the myriad of restaurants, the event typifies this vibrant, dynamic area of the city and its traditions. It also speaks of a fierce pride of community.

Asian pioneers were initially lured to Canada by the Caribou gold rush and the opportunities for employment offered by the construction of the Canadian Pacific Railway. During this Victorian era of colonialism, however, the Asian community was not readily accepted by the white majority. Viewed as a major threat to the labour market, Chinese were subjected to substantial derision and abuse, which culminated in serious and violent anti-Asian demonstrations in 1887 and 1907.

Despite the difficulties, the Asian community survived and prospered as a distinctive entity around the area of West Pender Street. Following a long cultural tradition, the earliest "Chinatown" housed open-air shops and markets, baths, gambling centres, and a few opium dens. Indeed, opium production for export was a respected, legal enterprise in Canada at the time and this product became one of the west coast's first major exports to the United States.

The tenacity of the Asian culture in the face of occasionally oppressive circumstances was also reflected in the distinctive architectural style of the area. A walk through Chinatown today will illustrate the recessed balconies, the intricate woodworking, and the ornamental wrought iron which distinguished the Asian part of the city. That unique atmosphere continues to prevail, making Vancouver's Chinatown a distinctive addition to the tapestry of the city.

FALSE CREEK

WHEN THE EARLY COLONISTS first arrived in the Vancouver area, they discovered a diminutive cousin to the giant Burrard Inlet. Called False Creek, this smaller inlet swept some five kilometres inland, connecting with the Burrard Inlet during high tide.

Despite its small size, False Creek became the industrial heart of the city. The Canadian Pacific Railway built its first terminal at the base of Granville Street, near the entrance of the inlet.

Industries requiring water and transportation rapidly followed. However, the industrial sludge, sewage, and the natural decay of ocean vegetation combined to produce a rather odorous area of the city. Noise was often deafening; visually the area was unimpressive.

Relief came, however, when the Government of Canada was secure in the survival of the C.P.R. and permitted the construction of a second railway in

1915. The Canadian Pacific Northern Railway filled in close to one-third of the inlet in order to build its terminus.

With industrial demand for land constantly growing, infilling became the primary means through which the need could be met. In 1915 an artificial island known as Granville Island was created by dredging the inlet.

Industry remained the backbone of False Creek for

Granville Island.

decades. However, as industry became less dependent on rail transport and as new industrial parks outside of Vancouver became more prevalent, False Creek gradually declined. The deterioration of the area spurred a massive redevelopment program in the early 1970s. The results are impressive.

Much of the area is now residential—a combination of new condominiums, townhouses, apartments, and restored older buildings intermixed to create distinctive neighborhoods.

The industrial island of Granville has been converted into one of the major recreational areas of the city while still retaining some of its industries. Old warehouses and factories have been transformed into restaurants, theatres, and a public market offering a range of fresh produce for the shopper.

Across the water the newest addition to the False Creek waterfront is the spectacular, multimillion dollar 1986 World Exposition. Focusing upon the theme "World in Motion—World in Touch," Expo 86 is a signal that Vancouver has truly come of age.

The site of Expo 86 offers a bright and vibrant focal point for Vancouver's centennial celebrations.

THE WEST END

THE DREAMERS were at it again.....

It was not enough that John Morton, his cousin Samuel Brighouse and friend William Hailstone had wasted their time searching for gold in the interior of the province. Now the three young Englishmen had wasted $500.55 on the purchase of 222 hectares of land to build (of all things) a brick factory using the clay deposits in the area. In 1862, with the finest forests in the world towering over them, the gamble seemed like folly. The "three greenhorns," it was assumed, were about to lose their money.

As it turned out, the brick-making factory could not compete with the cheaper lumber and did indeed prove a failure. The land, however, became some of the most highly valued real estate in Canada, supporting one of the most densely populated areas in the country.

One-third of the "brick makers" claim ended up in C.P.R. hands as part of the negotiated land grant. It was upon this property that the railway developed the highly prized estates of "Blueblood Alley." The beaches of English Bay and the beauty of Stanley Park made this a most attractive area for those of wealth and position.

During the boom years around the turn of the century, the demand for housing on the peninsula grew so great that the large estates of the West End rapidly gave way to a proliferation of apartment buildings. So rapid was the transformation from a low-density to high-density district that, in 1920, city officials imposed a six-story limit on buildings to restrain the effects of rapid development.

These height restrictions proved adequate until after the Second World War. With this new postwar demand, an expanding complex of highrises began to stretch skyward once more. A new forest of concrete began to replace the once-mighty stands of Douglas-fir.

Despite its dense population, the West End is a strong community. Residents are very proud of the friendly atmosphere and many community organizations. A great variety of neighborhood shops and restaurants add to the enjoyment of this most pleasant region.

The West End is an interesting mixture of small, single-family homes remaining from the early years, apartment blocks of not

more than six stories, dating from the 1920s, and the large
highrise apartment buildings of more recent decades. West End
residents enjoy close proximity to the beaches of English Bay
and the relaxing forests, gardens and views of Stanley Park.

37

PARKS AND GARDENS

EVEN DURING THE earliest years, Vancouver citizens looked upon the natural environment as an essential component of their quality of life. Chief among their prized possessions is spectacular Stanley Park. At 404 hectares, it is the second largest civic park in North America after New York's Central Park.

The area became a Military Reserve in 1863, after a series of disputes with the U.S. over the San Juan Islands. In 1888, the military lands were transformed into park lands. Named after Lord Stanley of Preston, then the governor general of Canada, the park became a haven for Vancouverites, who fiercely protected their small bit of wilderness paradise.

Stanley Park today offers that same respite from the heightened pace of city living. With 43 kilometres of footpaths and bicycle trails, and a continuous granite seawall around the shoreline, the park allows for both exercise and quiet reflection.

As well as its natural beauty, the park offers a wide variety of recreational opportunities. The Vancouver Aquarium, the largest in Canada, houses close to 9,000 species of sea life including several types of sea mammals. Spotlighted are the unique capabilities of resident killer whales (orcas) and beluga whales. Land mammals are featured in the Stanley Park Zoo, and children have the opportunity to interact with animals firsthand in a special, smaller centre created specifically for them.

The list of attractions is seemingly endless; tennis courts, miniature golf, Lost Lagoon, lawn bowling, an outdoor theatre, restaurants, sculptures, gardens, a swimming pool, and spectacular views of Burrard Inlet.

One feature of the park deserves special attention. There is an excellent collection of totem poles, fitting in a park which had been a seasonal home of the Coast Salish Indians for many centuries. Although these poles represent only one component of the artistic and cultural heritage of the native west coast peoples, they are remarkable examples of a society which developed over several thousand years prior to the arrival of the first white explorers.

Once regarded as the most beautiful facet of a rough and tumble frontier town, Stanley Park has remained a centrepiece of the community. Though Vancouver is now an attractive setting for the park, residents continue to value the opportunity to relax, explore and let problems slip away.

Stanley Park is the largest of Vancouver's park and recreational areas. With many kilometres of trails, beautiful vistas, and a wide array of attractions such as the Vancouver Aquarium, it is understandable that residents, for close to a century, have viewed Stanley Park as the centrepiece of their community.

An old abandoned quarry site has been reclaimed as beautiful gardens in Queen Elizabeth Park.

Vancouver is also noted for a spectacular array of landscaped botanical gardens and park areas. One may choose from the tranquil serenity of the traditional Japanese displays of the Nitobe Memorial Gardens at the University of British Columbia, or wander through one of Canada's most comprehensive collection of plants at the 22-hectare Van Dusen Botanical Gardens.

Located on the highest point of land in Vancouver, Queen Elizabeth Park is unrivalled for the scenic view alone. Although a mere 122 metres above sea level, the summit of "Little Mountain" offers a breathtaking 360-degree panorama of the city, Burrard Inlet, and the mountain backdrop. A triodatic dome, donated by the Bloedel family, crowns the mountain and houses plants of the tropics, semitropics, and the desert.

The Bloedel Conservatory on the summit of "Little Mountain."

UNIVERSITY OF BRITISH COLUMBIA

THE UNIVERSITY OF British Columbia—the province's oldest and largest university—was approved in principle by the provincial legislature in 1908. Three years later, 1,214 hectares of the Point Grey Peninsula were set aside as endowment lands, the sale of which was to help fund development. Despite this economic support, events repeatedly interrupted construction of the campus. More than a decade after construction had been initiated, classes were still being held in a small cluster of huts far from the Point Grey site. Frustration built to a point where both students and faculty joined in the "Great Trek" of 1922 to spur speedier completion of the campus. The protest march was successful and in 1925 the U.B.C. campus officially opened its doors.

The university has a wonderful range of architectural styles beginning with the earliest Modern Tudor buildings designed to reflect British scholastic institutions. Later structures from the 1950s adopt the more precise, linear design characteristic of the International style.

Perhaps the most intriguing building, however, is the spectactular design of the Museum of Anthropology, created by Arthur Erikson. Based upon traditional northwest coast Indian buildings, the museum houses a fascinating array of exhibits and artifacts. It is a stop not to be missed.

The U.B.C. campus.

Museum of Anthropology at the University of British Columbia.

KITSILANO

ALTHOUGH THE C.P.R. claimed ownership of the Kitsilano area as early as 1884, the area did not truly begin its growth until after the completion of the second Granville Street bridge in 1909 and the establishment of streetcar lines in the area. Named after Chief Khahtsahlano of the Squamish tribe, "Kits" became popular as a less expensive alternative to the West End. In recent years, however, the streets of small homes have gradually been giving way to apartment blocks.

Kitsilano is best known for its spectacular beach areas. Indeed, even prior to the construction of the bridge, many Vancouver residents would row their boats to these quieter beaches away from crowded English Bay.

In addition to these park areas, Kitsilano offers a number of other sights, including the H. R. MacMillan Planetarium, guarded by George Norris's crab sculpture, the Vancouver Maritime Museum, and one of the city's oldest symbols of its past—the Hastings Mill store, built around 1865.

Jericho Beach.

Kitsilano Beach with the West End of Vancouver in the background.

The crab sculpture outside the Vancouver Planetarium.

43

NORTH ACROSS THE WATER

SUSAN MOODY MADE it very clear; Moodyville was not about to suffer the uncivilized alcoholic behavior seen across the water. This town was to remain loyal to the company, and the company would, in time, provide a wide array of services and facilities for the residents.

The residents complied; Moodyville became a well-behaved company town and the Moodys kept their promises. During the 1860s and 1870s, Moodyville was briefly the most important community along the Burrard Inlet, offering such things as the first school and the first electric lighting. Despite this, the community remained isolated and quite separate from the intense activity on the opposite shore. Even as the North Shore communities grew up around the nucleus of the Moody lumber mill, the tradition of separateness endured. Unlike South Vancouver, the independent municipalities of North and West Vancouver have refrained from joining the huge metropolis across the inlet.

West Vancouver is a rare municipality in that it very early decided to ban industrial development. It remains solely a residential area relying upon homeowners and service industries to supply the necessary tax base. It was this ban on industry which helped to attract the Guinness brewing family to invest in the North Shore. For a meagre sum of $75,000, 1,618 hectares of land were purchased and transformed into the elite estates called the British Properties. Isolation proved to be a problem, however, and the Guinness family constructed the spectacular Lions Gate Bridge in 1938 to provide easy access to the city of Vancouver. A toll was charged until the city purchased the bridge in 1963.

Lions Gate Bridge is named for the mountains called "the lions," visible to the north.

From its beginnings North Vancouver welcomed industry, and today it relies heavily on lumber, grain-handling and shipbuilding to support the city. It also provides all lower mainland residents with some of their prime recreational havens.

Amongst the best known is Grouse Mountain, a year-round attraction. Aerial tramways carry visitors to 1,128 metres for skiing in winter and spectacular sightseeing in the summer.

The Capilano River, the boundary between north and south, provides the water supply for the lower mainland. By carefully protecting the watershed, the city has ensured water so pure that it requires very little treatment. This protection also allows visitors to witness a natural phenomenon of the west coast—the annual salmon run. The Capilano fish hatchery and the Capilano suspension bridge are two spots which visitors to the North Shore should not miss.

View of North Vancouver from the city of Vancouver.

The Royal Hudson train.

Copyright ©1986 by Whitecap Books Ltd.

Canadian Cataloguing in Publication Data

Bondar, Barry
 Vancouver chronicles

 ISBN 0-920620-92-2

 1. Vancouver (B.C.) - History. 2.
Vancouver (B.C.) - Description - Guide-books.
3. Vancouver (B.C.) - Description - Views.
I. Title.
FC3847.3.B65 1986 917.11'33 C86-091223-X
F1089.5.V22B65 1986

Typeset by The Typeworks, Vancouver, B.C.

Printed by D.W. Friesen & Sons, Altona, Manitoba,
Canada

Published by Whitecap Books, 1086 West 3rd Street,
North Vancouver, B.C.

Photo Credits

Front cover: Chris Speedie, Photo/Graphics
Back cover: Provincial Archives of B.C., HP 31854
pp. 2—23: The Provincial Archives of B.C.
 p.2: HP 9120; p.3: HP 39729; p.4: HP 79470; p.5:
 HP 37820; p.6: HP 70398; p.7 top: HP 9116,
 bottom: HP 9144; p.8: HP 37201; p.9: HP 9159;
 p.10: HP 9278; p.11: HP 911; p.12: HP 845; p.13:
 HP 9192; p.14: HP 41295; p.15: HP 66243; p.15: HP
 9112(b); p.16: HP 71018; p.17 top: HP 75726,
 bottom: HP 32260; p.18: HP 41714; p.19 top: HP
 33128, bottom: HP 32265; p.20/21: HP 70817; p.21:
 HP 65998; p.22/23: HP 40072

p.24/25: Rick Marotz, Photo/Graphics; p.26: Gunter Marx,
Photo/Graphics; p.27: T. Sloan, Photo/Graphics; p.29: Jurgen
Vogt, Photo/Graphics; p.29 top: Gunter Marx, Photo/Graphics;
pp.30, upper, 31: Marin Petkov, Photo/Graphics; p.30 lower:
Michael Burch; p.33, upper: Jurgen Vogt, Photo/Graphics; p.33,
lower: Marin Petkov, Photo/Graphics; p.32/33: Gunter Marx,
Photo/Graphics; p.34, 35, 36/37: Jurgen Vogt, Photo/Graphics;
p.38, 39: Bob Herger, Photo/Graphics; p.40, upper: Fred Chapman,
Photo/Graphics; p.40, lower: Marin Petkov, Photo/Graphics; p.41,
top: Tony Gibson, Photo/Graphics; p.41, bottom left: Fred
Chapman, Photo/Graphics; p.41, bottom right: Gunter Marx,
Photo/Graphics; p.42: Jurgen Vogt, Photo/Graphics; p.43: Derek &
Jane Abson, Photo/Graphics; p.42/43: Gunter Marx,
Photo/Graphics; p.44: Roger Laurilla, Photo/Graphics; p.45:
Michael Burch; p.46: Marin Petkov, Photo/Graphics; pp.46/47:
Gunter Marx; p.48: Michael Burch